The · Life Cycle · Series

The Life Cycle of a

Honeybee

Bobbie Kalman

Crabtree Publishing Company

www.crabtreebooks.com

The Life Cycle Series

A Bobbie Kalman Book

Dedicated by Margaret Amy Reiach
To Kara Green — the busiest of workers and the sweetest of friends.

Author and Editor-in-Chief
Bobbie Kalman

Research
Katherine Balpataky

Substantive editors
Amanda Bishop
Kathryn Smithyman

Editors
Molly Aloian
Kelley MacAulay
Rebecca Sjonger

Art director
Robert MacGregor

Design
Margaret Amy Reiach

Production coordinator
Heather Fitzpatrick

Photo research
Crystal Foxton

Consultant
Patricia Loesche, Ph.D., Animal Behavior Program,
Department of Psychology, University of Washington

Photographs
Diane Payton Majumdar: front cover (honeybee)
© stephenmcdaniel.com: title page, pages 7, 8, 9, 10, 12,
    14 (top), 15, 16, 17, 19, 20, 21, 22, 23, 24, 26, 27, 28, 30, 31
Visuals Unlimited: Bill Beatty: page 4;
    R. Williamson/L.J. Connor: page 13;
    E.S. Ross: page 14 (bottom);
    William J. Weber: pages 18, 25;
    Inga Spence: page 29
Other images by Digital Vision

Illustrations
Margaret Amy Reiach: pages 11 (bottom and right),
    25 (bottom)
Bonna Rouse: front and back cover, series logo, title page,
    pages 5, 6-7, 8, 9, 10, 11 (top and left), 12, 14, 15, 16, 17, 18,
    22, 23, 25 (top), 27, 28, 29, 30, 31

Digital prepress
Embassy Graphics

Printer
Worzalla Publishing

Crabtree Publishing Company

www.crabtreebooks.com   1-800-387-7650

PMB 16A
350 Fifth Avenue
Suite 3308
New York, NY
10118

612 Welland Avenue
St. Catharines
Ontario
Canada
L2M 5V6

73 Lime Walk
Headington
Oxford
OX3 7AD
United Kingdom

Cataloging-in-Publication Data
Kalman, Bobbie.
   The life cycle of a honeybee / Bobbie Kalman.
      p. cm. -- (The life cycle series)
   Includes index.
   ISBN 0-7787-0664-8 (RLB) -- ISBN 0-7787-0694-X (pbk.)
   1. Honeybee--Life cycles--Juvenile literature. [1. Honeybee. 2. Bees.]
I. Title.
   QL568.A6K35 2004
   595.79'9--dc22
                                                        2003027233
                                                              LC

Contents

What is a honeybee?

A honeybee is an **insect**. Insects are **invertebrates**, or animals with no backbones. Instead, they have hard coverings called **exoskeletons** on the outsides of their bodies. Unlike many other insects, honeybees are **social**. They live in **colonies**, or groups. Each colony of honeybees builds a **hive** in which to live.

*There are over 25,000 different **species**, or kinds, of bees. Only eight bee species are honeybees. This book describes the life cycle of a western or common honeybee.*

drone

worker

queen

Types of honeybees

There are three types of honeybees: **workers**, **drones**, and **queens**. Worker bees are female. They are the smallest honeybees. Workers have many jobs. They build, clean, and protect the hive, care for young bees, and **groom**, or clean, the queen. Workers also collect pollen and nectar outside the hive, which they make into food for the entire colony!

Drones are male honeybees. They spend most of their time inside the hive, but they do not work. Their only job is to **mate**, or join together with a queen to make babies. Only one queen lives in each colony. She is the largest honeybee. The queen lays all the eggs from which new honeybees will **hatch**.

There are usually several thousand workers in a hive, but there are very few drones.

Busy body

A honeybee's body is made up of three sections: a head; a **thorax**, or midsection; and an **abdomen**, or lower body. Each section has many important parts.

The different body parts of a honeybee have special **functions**, or jobs. Look at the diagram below to learn how a honeybee's body works.

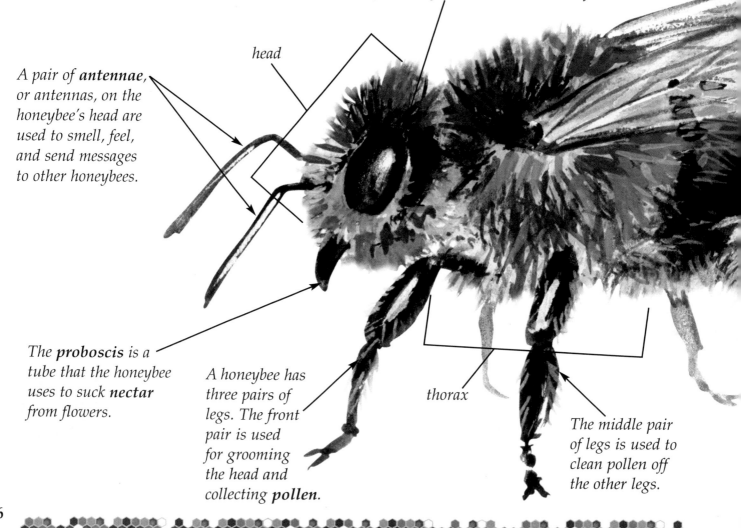

*A honeybee has five eyes! There are three small eyes at the front of its head and two large **compound eyes**, one on either side of its head.*

head

*A pair of **antennae**, or antennas, on the honeybee's head are used to smell, feel, and send messages to other honeybees.*

*The **proboscis** is a tube that the honeybee uses to suck **nectar** from flowers.*

*A honeybee has three pairs of legs. The front pair is used for grooming the head and collecting **pollen**.*

thorax

The middle pair of legs is used to clean pollen off the other legs.

Bee family tree

Honeybees belong to a group of insects called *Hymenoptera*, which includes ants, wasps, and other bees. All these insects have wings that are thin enough to see through. As a honeybee flies, its wings move rapidly. Honeybees can fly as fast as 15 miles per hour (24 km/h).

A honeybee has a pair of wings on its thorax.

— abdomen

*Each hind leg has a special part called a **pollen basket**. See page 25 for more information.*

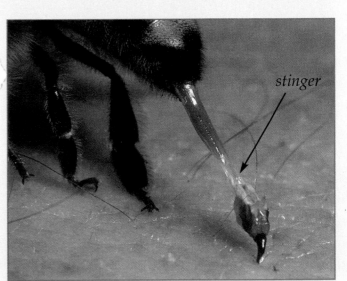

stinger

Sting operation

Female honeybees have **stingers** that they use for protection. They poke the stingers into their enemies and pump in **venom**, or poison. Workers can use their stingers only once. When a worker flies away, its stinger tears away from its body. Workers die shortly after stinging, but a queen's stinger never comes off after stinging. Her stinger is also an **ovipositor**, or a tube she uses to lay eggs.

Where do honeybees live?

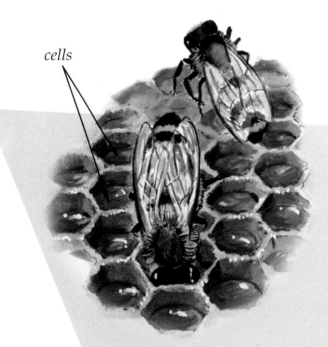

cells

The cells in a hive are used for many purposes, including storing food.

A honeybee hive is a busy place! It is very well built to meet all the needs of the colony. Each hive is a nest, a home, and a food factory all in one.

Making beeswax

Hives are made from **beeswax**, which is a substance that honeybees produce with their bodies. Workers shed the wax in flakes. They soften the flakes with **saliva** and shape the wax using their front legs and **mandibles**, or mouthparts.

Beat for heat

The workers beat their wings as they work. Heat from their moving muscles warms the air in the hive. Wax is easy to shape at a high temperature. The workers keep the hive at an ideal temperature—about 95 degrees Fahrenheit (35°C).

Tough cell

Once the wax is prepared, the workers get busy! They build the wax into **hexagonal**, or six-sided, cells. This shape makes the cells strong enough to support up to 25 times their own weight! There are about 100,000 cells in one hive. They are tightly packed together to form a **comb**, or sheet of cells. The cells are placed side by side and back to back, so that no space is wasted between them.

In the hive

The cells in a hive have different uses. The cells near the center of the hive are used to raise young honeybees. Cells around the center cells store food. Day and night, thousands of workers scurry over the many cells in the hive to make sure that every job is being done.

*Some honeybees live in hives that are made for them by people called **beekeepers**. For more on beekeepers, see page 27.*

What is a life cycle?

All animals go through a set of changes called a **life cycle**. First, they are born or they hatch from eggs. They then grow and change into adults. As adults, animals can make babies. When a baby is born, a new life cycle begins.

Here for a short time

An animal's life cycle is not the same as its **life span**. A life span is the length of time an animal is alive. The three types of honeybees have different life spans, and honeybees born in the spring have shorter life spans than those born in the fall. Workers live between 20 and 340 days, depending on when they are born. Drones live between 20 and 90 days. Queens live longer than drones and workers. They may live as long as four to five years, no matter what time of the year they were born!

From egg to adult

Honeybees begin their life cycles in eggs. **Larvae**, or larvas, hatch from the eggs. The larvae soon begin their **metamorphosis**, or total body change. They become **pupae**, or pupas. Metamorphosis is complete when the pupae become adults. Adult honeybees are **mature**, or fully developed.

The length of time it takes to complete these stages is different for each type of honeybee. It takes a worker about 21 days to complete its life cycle. A drone takes up to 24 days. A queen's life cycle lasts only about 15 days. When the queen lays eggs, a new life cycle begins with each egg.

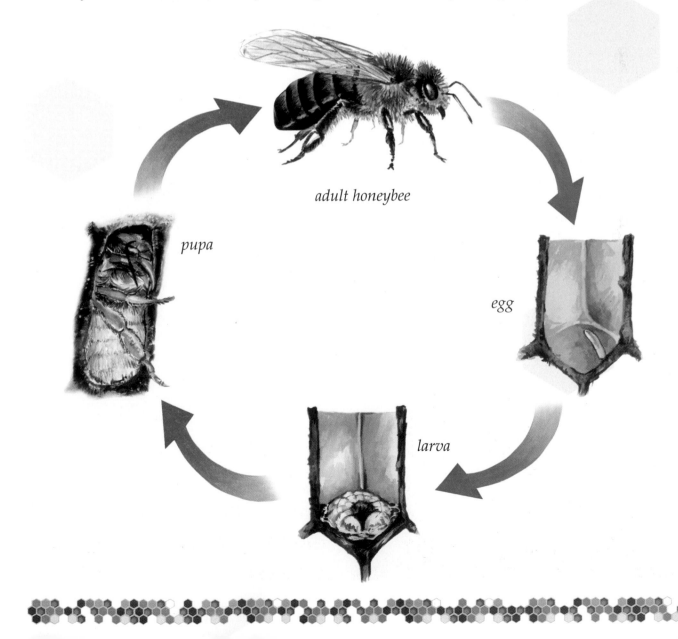

adult honeybee

pupa

egg

larva

The perfect place

All the eggs in a hive are laid by the queen of the colony. There are always many eggs in the hive because the queen lays up to 1,500 per day! Each day, she searches the hive for empty **brood cells,** or cells in which she can lay eggs. She uses only cells that have been thoroughly cleaned by the workers.

The queen lays a single egg inside each brood cell. The egg is attached to the cell wall with a sticky substance called **mucus**. Inside the egg is a tiny honeybee **embryo** and a **yolk**. The yolk is the food that the embryo will eat.

Each honeybee egg is only about one-sixteenth of an inch (0.2 cm) long.

Free at last!

After three days, the egg hatches. The new honeybee larva does not break out of its **egg membrane**, or soft shell, as other animal babies do. Instead, the egg membrane **dissolves**, or slowly breaks down into liquid. The newly hatched larva looks very similar to the egg in shape, size, and color.

The honeybees that hatch from these eggs will stay in their cells throughout the first three stages of their life cycles.

Little larvae

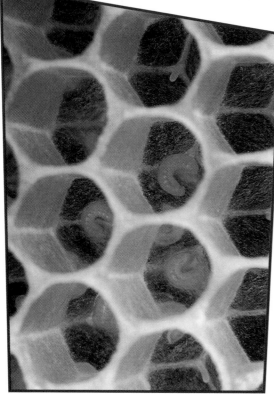

The larva stage lasts six to eight days for queens, six days for workers, and six to seven days for drones.

Honeybee larvae have no eyes, wings, legs, or antennae because they do not yet need these parts. The larva stage of the life cycle is about only one thing—eating! The larvae eat as much as they can in order to grow bigger. If they do not eat the proper types and amounts of food, they may become small adults or have shorter-than-normal life spans.

Chow down

Tiny white larvae feed constantly on food that is brought by workers called **nurse bees**. The nurse bees feed the larvae a mixture called **brood food**. It contains substances from the workers' bodies as well as water and honey, which only honeybees make. As the larvae get older, they may also feed on **bee bread**, a mixture of honey and pollen that has been prepared as food. Each larva receives hundreds of small meals a day from the nurse bees.

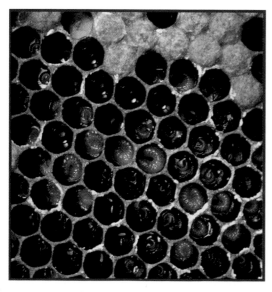

Food fit for a queen

Queen larvae eat a special type of brood food called **royal jelly**. This substance has more honey than other types of brood food. The queen is fed royal jelly—and a lot of it—throughout her entire life cycle.

A queen larva, shown right, is slightly larger than a drone larva, whereas a worker larva is slightly smaller than a drone larva.

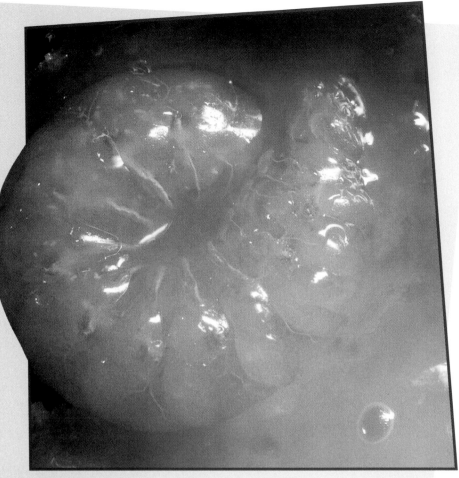

Skintight

The larvae feed and grow constantly for several days, but their skins do not grow with their bodies. The larvae must **molt**, or shed their skins, so that their bodies will have enough room to grow bigger. When a larva has molted four times, workers create a wax **cap**, or cover, over its cell and seal it shut. After its cell has been capped, the larva stretches out its body and spins a **cocoon**, or silk case, around itself. The larva spends the next few days inside the cocoon, where it begins its metamorphosis.

To be a bee...

While in the cocoon, the honeybee changes from a larva to a pupa. The new pupa's body is almost fully developed, except for its wings. Its color grows darker, and its insides change. The pupa then completes the fifth and final molt of its life cycle. This last molt changes it into an adult honeybee.

A drone pupa (above) molts one last time to become an adult (below).

Bursting out

The new adult's body is soft, so the honeybee must wait in its capped cell for several hours while its body hardens. When the honeybee is ready, it carefully chews the edge of the wax cap to separate it from the cell wall. The workers then collect the wax caps and reuse them elsewhere in the hive.

Out in the open

When the honeybee finally struggles out of its cell, it stretches out its antennae and wings and waits for the hairs on its body to dry. Workers then bring food to the young adult and begin grooming it.

This new adults has just crawled out of its cell. Now it must rest for a while. Workers gather around the new adult. They will look after it until it is able to look after itself.

Fully grown

The new adult honeybees may look very different than they did as larvae, but they are still very hungry! Workers, drones, and queens all need plenty of food in their first days as adults. Their bodies look fully grown, but their insides continue to develop for the next few days. In order to be healthy adults, workers eat pollen and honey, drones eat brood food, and queens continue to eat royal jelly. A successful colony needs healthy adults.

On this busy comb, the queen is easy to spot. A beekeeper has marked her with a blue tag.

Working for a living

Healthy adult queens and drones ensure that many eggs are laid. Most eggs develop into workers. Workers run the hive. Their jobs change as they get older, so workers in all stages of development are necessary to the hive. In the first days of her life, a worker cleans cells and helps keep the brood cells warm. She then becomes a nurse bee. Her job is to help feed larvae.

After that, she helps build the hive and carry food and wax wherever it is needed. Next, she becomes a **guard bee**. Guard bees protect the entrance to the hive. The last days of the worker's life are spent as a **field bee**. Field bees leave the hive to gather nectar and pollen. They then bring the nectar and pollen back to the hive to be made into food for the entire colony.

Guard bees inspect every animal that tries to enter the hive, as shown above. If an intruder such as a wasp or moth tries to enter, the guard bees release a special **scent**, *or smell, to alert the colony. They then flap their wings, kick their legs, bite, or sting to stop the intruder.*

Mating

When the queen is mature, she prepares to mate with a drone. Mature drones produce a fluid called **sperm** in their bodies. Sperm is used for **reproduction**, or making babies. It **fertilizes** the eggs that are inside the queen's body.

On the move

When the queen is ready to mate, she leaves the hive and flies to a mating area chosen by the drones. Here, she may mate with 15 to 20 drones before she returns to the hive. She stores their sperm in her body, so she will not need to mate again for the rest of her life. The drones do not live long after they have mated.

When drones are ready to mate, they leave the hive and wait for a queen to meet them.

Eggs for workers and drones

The queen returns to the hive after mating and immediately begins laying eggs. **Fertilized eggs**, or eggs that have come into contact with sperm, hatch into female workers. **Unfertilized eggs** are eggs that have never come into contact with the sperm of the drones. These eggs hatch into drones.

Only special eggs hatch into queens. Turn to page 22 to learn more about queen eggs.

A new hive

The first queen to leave her cell usually kills the other queens by stinging them through their wax caps.

Most hives have one queen and enough room for only a certain number of honeybees. When the hive becomes too crowded, many of the honeybees prepare to **swarm**, or leave the hive as a group. Some of the workers build special queen brood cells, which are larger than regular brood cells. They feed the larvae royal jelly.

And they're off!

When the developing queens are almost ready to leave their brood cells, the colony's old queen flies away. She is followed by thousands of workers. The honeybees that stay in the hive wait for the first developing queen to crawl out of her cell. She becomes the colony's new queen.

A swarm leaves the hive and gathers nearby.

Out in the open

The swarming honeybees set out to find a new home. First, they gather on a large object, such as a tree branch. A few workers called **scout bees** begin searching for a good **nest site**, or spot for the new hive. They may spend hours or even days trying to find a spot that is safely out of sight, such as a hollow tree or a crack in a wall. When the scout bees have found a good site, they return to the swarm and do a dance to tell the colony where to find it. As soon as the swarm reaches the new nest site, the honeybees begin building a hive.

In North America, honeybees swarm in May or June to give them enough time to build a new hive, mate, and prepare for winter.

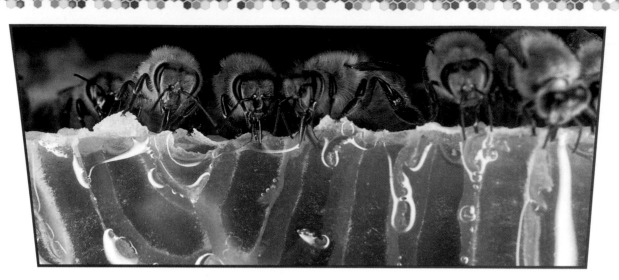

Honeybee feasts

Workers have to find a lot of food in order to feed the whole colony. They make many kinds of food, but they are most famous for their honey. Only honeybees can use nectar from flowers to make honey. How do they do it?

Finding nectar

Workers **cooperate**, or work together, to locate food. When one worker finds a good food source, it uses its proboscis to reach inside the flower and suck out the flower's nectar. The honeybee then returns to the hive to let the other workers know where to find the food.

Home delivery

A field bee collects nectar in its **honey stomach**, a special body part used to store food. When its honey stomach is full, the worker carries the nectar back to the hive. It gives the nectar to other workers. These workers then make the nectar into food.

Shake it up!

Honeybees use movement to communicate with the rest of the colony. When field bees return to the hive after searching for food, they use special movements to tell the other workers where the food can be found. They do a **round dance** to show that nectar is close by. When nectar is far away, field bees do a **waggle dance** to describe the distance to the nectar and the direction in which it can be found.

waggle dance

round dance

Good partners

Honeybees eat pollen to get **protein**. Field bees collect pollen from flowers. They store it in pollen baskets on their legs. When the baskets are full, the field bees return to the hive and store the pollen in food cells. Extra pollen often sticks to their body hairs and antennae. This pollen is carried to all the other plants a honeybee visits. Pollen movement is important because many plants need pollen from other plants of their species in order to reproduce. Honeybees **pollinate** plants by carrying grains of pollen from one plant to another.

pollen basket

The season ends

Drones do not live in the hive during winter. If a drone egg is laid, the workers will eat it. If a drone larva emerges, workers drag it out of the hive. Adult drones are not fed, so they soon die.

When winter comes, the air is too cold for honeybees. They must spend the coldest months inside the hive. They cannot leave the hive to collect food. The workers prepare for winter by making plenty of extra food. The queen lays fewer eggs at this time, so there is room to store the food.

Keeping out the cold

As the temperature outside the hive drops, workers seal up any cracks in the hive. They use sticky plant substances called **gums** to seal every spot that might let in cold air. When the hive has been sealed, the workers huddle together. They start shaking their wing muscles, causing their bodies give off heat. The heat warms the hive. The workers keep moving their wings until spring, when the air grows warm again.

Keepers of the bees

A colony stores up to three times as much honey as it will need for winter. For hundreds of years, beekeepers have **harvested**, or safely gathered, extra honey from hives. They sell the honey as food. They also harvest wax, royal jelly, and even venom! These substances are used in medicines that treat human diseases.

An apiary

Humans cannot get into natural hives easily, so beekeepers build their own hives and put colonies in them. A wooden hive is called an **apiary**. Each apiary has wooden trays with cells in which the honeybees store their honey. At harvest time, the beekeeper puts on a protective suit, removes the trays, and collects the extra honey and wax.

*Beekeepers keep several honeybee colonies in wooden trays called **skeps**.*

27

Dangers to honeybees

Today, honeybees face many dangers. There are few wild honeybee populations left in North America. Honeybees are **endangered** in many countries. Endangered species are at risk of dying out.

A good site is hard to find

Most of the honeybee colonies in the world today are kept by beekeepers in specially built hives. Wild honeybees must find their own nest sites, but good sites are becoming hard to find. Loss of **habitat**, or natural places in which to live, makes it difficult for swarms to find new homes.

Wildflowers

Honeybees and plants need each other to survive. Without plant nectar and pollen, honeybees would have no food. If the honeybees did not pollinate the plants, many would not be able to reproduce. As land is developed for buildings, roads, and farms, wild plants have fewer places in which to grow. As the wildflowers disappear, so do wild honeybees.

Introduced pests

Sometimes, a species from one part of the world is **introduced**, or brought into, another animal's habitat. Honeybees are threatened by introduced species such as wax moths and varroa mites. Wax moths are from Russia. They find their way into hives and lay their eggs inside. When the moth eggs hatch, the larvae damage the hives by eating beeswax and honey. Varroa mites are from Asia. They are tiny bugs that live on honeybees and feed on their eggs and larvae. Scientists around the world are studying wax moths and varroa mites to find ways to protect honeybees.

Many honeybees die because they collect pollen from flowers that have been sprayed with **pesticides***. These chemicals are used to kill pests, but they kill helpful insects too. A garden without chemicals is safest for all living things.*

Helping honeybees

*Some people are **allergic** to honeybee venom. They must take precautions to avoid being stung. Most honeybees will not sting unless they are threatened, however.*

Honeybees are amazing creatures that do a lot to help people. Anyone who likes to eat delicious golden honey or admire wildflowers knows how important honeybees are. You can help by telling other people why honeybees are an important part of the natural world.

Let the honeybees be!

When natural places are protected, honeybees are able to find the plants they need for food and the spots they need for nesting without bothering humans. Convince your family, friends, and neighbors to avoid wild honeybees and their hives. Encourage people you know to plant more trees and flowers. Ask your parents to keep your family's garden and yard free of pesticides and any other chemicals, which can hurt honeybees and other animals.

You can support beekeepers in your community by buying their honey and other products.

Get the buzz on honeybees!

Learn all you can about these unbee-lievable little animals! An Internet search can get you going, or you can check out these great websites:

- www.pbs.org/wgbh/nova/bees
- www.pbs.org/wnet/nature/alienempire/multimedia/hive.html
- www.honey.com/kids/index.html

Glossary

Note: Boldfaced words that are defined in the text may not appear in the glossary.

allergic Describing a person whose body reacts negatively to a substance such as honeybee venom

beekeeper A person who raises bees

compound eyes Eyes that are made up of thousands of tiny lenses

drone A male honeybee

embryo An animal that is developing inside an egg

fertilize To add sperm to an egg

hatch To complete the first stage of a life cycle by emerging from an egg

hive The home of a honeybee colony

insect An animal with no backbone and six legs

nectar A sweet liquid found in flowers

pesticide A chemical that kills insects

pollen A substance produced by plants for reproduction

protein A substance that makes an animal's body stronger

queen The only female in a honeybee colony that makes babies

saliva A liquid that breaks down food

social Describing animals that live in groups

worker A female honeybee that works constantly to maintain the hive and care for young honeybees

Index

1 2 3 4 5 6 7 8 9 0   Printed in the U.S.A.   3 2 1 0 9 8 7 6 5 4